This Book Belongs to

_____

Getting to Know Yourself, Do You Know You?

Copyright © 2021 by Jazmine Stevenson

All rights reserved. No part of this publication may be reproduced, distributed, or transmitted in any form or by any means, including photocopying, recording, or other electronic or mechanical methods, without the prior written permission of the publisher, except in the case of brief quotations embodied in critical reviews and certain other noncommercial uses permitted by copyright law. For permission requests, write to the publisher, addressed "Attention: Permissions Coordinator," at the address below.

Independent Authors Publications
P.O Box 7062
Roselle, NJ 07203
www.independentauthorspublications.com

Books may be ordered through booksellers or publisher by contacting us on our website.

Printed in the United States of America First Printing, 2021

Book Cover Design – Web Printlab
Editor – Catherine Felegi
Book Formatter – Web Printlab

ISBN 978-1-950974-06-1 (paperback)

Because of the dynamic nature of the Internet, any Web addresses or links contained in this book may have changed since the publication and may no longer be valid. The views expressed in this work are solely those of the author and do not necessarily reflect the views of the publisher, and the publisher hereby disclaims any responsibility for them.

TABLE OF CONTENTS

1. The Purpose of the Book — 5
2. Introduction — 6
3. Acknowledgements — 7-10
4. Know Yourself — 11-21
5. Be Compassionate to Yourself — 23-27
6. Release Self Doubt — 29-37
7. Accept Yourself — 39-43
8. Care for Yourself — 45-55
9. Love Yourself — 57-67
10. About the Author — 71

The Purpose of this Book

The purpose of this reflection workbook is to help you heal from past trauma that you may not even know about. In order to heal properly, you must know who you truly are. Most times when we are hurt, we make decisions based on our emotions. This can be dangerous.

For this workbook to help you heal, you MUST answer all questions honestly for YOURSELF.

Introduction

I was motivated to publish my own self-healing workbook because
I personally began to lose sight of who I am, and who's I am.
I was beginning to fall short of my full potential
and become depressed. I began
shying away from friends, family, myself, and even God.
During that dark moment, I knew I did not want to continue to feel that way. There was work
I needed to do within myself.
It was time to reflect.
I began this journey, and brought a few people along
to answer soul-searching questions with me.
Each week, I would text three or four questions to my circle.
They had a week to ponder.
Our group would then have a FaceTime "date" to answer the questions together.
It helped to hear the answers aloud.
Most times, we were very shocked by hearing our answers.
My friends and siblings noticed the
difference in our way of thinking by our answers, and our personal growth.
These questions have helped me look
at situations differently. I've learned how to
face obstacles with a new confidence.

Acknowledgements

I would like to give a special thank you to my support system,
everyone who has spoken into my life and pushed me.

God

I want to humbly thank You for Your covering.
My vision would not have been mine
if it weren't for Your guidance.
Lord, thank You for the push when I
wanted to give up.
Lord, Your grace and mercy is
appreciated beyond words.
Not only have You given me the vision,
But You blessed me with the best people in my life.
Lord, I stand here to thank You for
breaking my heart so I can run back to you.
I did not understand why You allowed
me to endure such pain at first,
but I understand now. I put people,
places, and things before You and that is why
things were not falling into place.
For You are a jealous God and I will not
allow myself to do such a thing again.
I am not deserving of Your favor but You insist on blessing me
with it.
I truly appreciate the unconditional love You have for me.
Lord, I pray this book and the books to come
will help others feel the need to PUSH,
to PRESS, and to LIVE!!

Dad

Thank you for being such an understanding, loving,
and wise man. Thank you for teaching me
that anything worth having will not
come easily. It may take some tears,
sleepless nights, and many talks with God.
It was necessary for me to do that.
My vision came from Him, and Him only!

Mom

Thank you for teaching me that fighting for what
I believe in is necessary. You have given me
the strength to stand up for myself
and accept nothing short of the best.

Parents

Thank you for your continued support and love. It will
never go unnoticed.
Thank you for investing so much time in me.
Without your time spent and sacrifices made, I would not
be half the woman I am today.
All of the struggles and pain you've gone through
do not go unseen. There aren't enough words

Siblings

Thank you for always being by my side, whether
physically or as a listening ear. You have helped
guide me and are all so true.
You are beautiful inside and out.
I am truly blessed to have you all in my life.

Closest Friends

Thank you for putting up with me
(I know I am a lot to handle).
Thank you for always being REAL with me!
Thank you for this LIFELONG friendship.

It's the quality for me!

I am forever thankful and blessed
beyond measure.
There isn't a moment when we talk that
you do not uplift me and bring
joy to my soul.
I LOVE YA FOR REAL!

Prophetess Karen Walkes

Ma Karen, I want to take the time to say thank you.
I know you are not here physically, but your spirit has been
living within me since you have gained your wings.
It would not be right if I did not mention you.
You deemed me your second child and took me
under your wing and acted as a profound mentor.
I hope I am making you proud.
I would trade anything in this world to hear that soft yet meaningful
voice again.
I want to stand here and tell everyone that I am forever thankful for
the love
and support that you have shown me while you were
physically on this earth.
You were so excited to see this day and I know you are
shining down on me and smiling that bright smile.

Auntie Overseer Dianne Martin

You've adopted me as your niece in 2020
and I am forever grateful.
It seems like I have grown up with you as my aunt.
You helped me step out of my comfort zone.
The weekly calls with me reading aloud
built a confidence in me I never knew I had.
You allowing me to speak about my
insecurities helped me in ways
you would never imagine.
Thank you!

Uncle Pastor John McArthur

Thank you for being who you are.
My uncle, who I adopted
in December 2019 (you did not have much
of a choice). In 2020, you showed me that
"uncle" was not just a title.
You always show up and show out.
I appreciate all of our talks,
even the ones I do not want hear at that
particular moment.
I did not know I needed someone so REAL
and RAW in my life until I met you.
The reason I felt the need to adopt you
was because I felt safe and protected.
Uncle...
YOU MATTER!

Know Yourself

It is imperative to learn about one's self. If you do not take the time alone getting to know yourself, you are more than likely going to settle and not know your worth. We are all valuable and should expect nothing short of the Best !

Getting to Know Yourself | 12

1. Research the meaning of your name. What is it? Do you feel you can live up to its meaning? How are you living up to it now?

_____
_____
_____
_____
_____
_____
_____
_____
_____
_____
_____
_____
_____
_____
_____
_____
_____

2. Using ten words or phrases, describe yourself.

1. _____
_____
2. _____
_____
3. _____
_____
4. _____
_____
5. _____
_____
6. _____
_____
7. _____
_____
8. _____
_____
9. _____
_____
10. _____
_____

3. What are some things you like about yourself? Why?

_____
_____
_____
_____
_____
_____
_____
_____
_____
_____
_____
_____
_____
_____
_____
_____

4. What are some things you don't like about yourself? Why?

_____
_____
_____
_____
_____
_____
_____
_____
_____
_____
_____
_____
_____
_____
_____
_____

5. Is there anything that you are passionate about? Name at least three things you are passionate about. Why are you passionate about them?

1. _____
_____
_____
_____
_____
_____

2. _____
_____
_____
_____
_____
_____

3. _____
_____
_____
_____
_____
_____

6. Do you have a favorite color? Look into the meaning of it. What is the symbolism behind it? Does this coincide with your personality?

_____
_____
_____
_____
_____
_____
_____
_____
_____
_____
_____
_____
_____
_____
_____
_____

7. What is your most memorable trait? What is so memorable about it?

_____
_____
_____
_____
_____
_____
_____
_____
_____
_____
_____
_____
_____
_____
_____

8. What are three things you are most proud of? Why?

1. _____
_____
_____
_____
_____
_____

2. _____
_____
_____
_____
_____
_____

3. _____
_____
_____
_____
_____
_____

9. What are your greatest skills and talents?

_____
_____
_____
_____
_____
_____
_____
_____
_____
_____
_____
_____
_____
_____
_____
_____

10. *What is one of your favorite memories?*

_____
_____
_____
_____
_____
_____
_____
_____
_____
_____
_____
_____
_____
_____
_____

Be Compassionate to Yourself

"We can't heal the world today but we can begin with a voice of compassion, a heart of love, and an act of kindness"
-Mary Davis

1. Have you embraced being uncomfortable? Explain why or why not.

_____
_____
_____
_____
_____
_____
_____
_____
_____
_____
_____
_____
_____
_____
_____
_____
_____

2. Have you ever been broken? What happened? Do you still feel that brokenness? Where do you think it stems from?

_____
_____
_____
_____
_____
_____
_____
_____
_____
_____
_____
_____
_____
_____
_____
_____
_____
_____

3. Describe a time that you felt anger. Do you still feel angered by circumstances in life? Why?

_____
_____
_____
_____
_____
_____
_____
_____
_____
_____
_____
_____
_____
_____
_____
_____
_____
_____

4. What are ways that you hold yourself accountable?

_____
_____
_____
_____
_____
_____
_____
_____
_____
_____
_____
_____
_____
_____
_____

Release Self Doubt

"I release fear, doubt and worry. I give myself permission to be happy"
-Rozine

1. Do you doubt yourself? Why? How often?

_____
_____
_____
_____
_____
_____
_____
_____
_____
_____
_____
_____
_____
_____
_____

2. What discourages you in life (can be about your career, life, your future, etc.)? Why do you allow the discouragement?

_____
_____
_____
_____
_____
_____
_____
_____
_____
_____
_____
_____
_____
_____
_____

3. What uplifts you? Why?

_____
_____
_____
_____
_____
_____
_____
_____
_____
_____
_____
_____
_____
_____
_____

4. What's something you like about yourself that you wish more people recognized?

_____
_____
_____
_____
_____
_____
_____
_____
_____
_____
_____
_____
_____
_____
_____
_____

5. What does success look like to you?

_____
_____
_____
_____
_____
_____
_____
_____
_____
_____
_____
_____
_____
_____
_____

6. What does success mean to you?

_____
_____
_____
_____
_____
_____
_____
_____
_____
_____
_____
_____
_____
_____
_____
_____

7. Have you ever experienced a miracle? If so, describe it.

_____
_____
_____
_____
_____
_____
_____
_____
_____
_____
_____
_____
_____
_____
_____

8. When you think of your childhood, what television shows and movies come to mind? List ten of them below.

1. _____
_____
2. _____
_____
3. _____
_____
4. _____
_____
5. _____
_____
6. _____
_____
7. _____
_____
8. _____
_____
9. _____
_____
10. _____
_____

Accept Yourself

"Take control of your destiny. Believe in yourself. Ignore those who try to discourage you. Avoid negative sources, People, Places and Habits"
-Lunaiah.com

1. Do you like who you are becoming? Why or why not?

_____
_____
_____
_____
_____
_____
_____
_____
_____
_____
_____
_____
_____
_____
_____

2. What goals, small or big, can you say you have achieved? List a few.

_____
_____
_____
_____
_____
_____
_____
_____
_____
_____
_____
_____
_____
_____
_____

3. Is there anything in life you take for granted? What is it? Why do you think you take it for granted?

_____
_____
_____
_____
_____
_____
_____
_____
_____
_____
_____
_____
_____
_____
_____
_____

4. Are you true to yourself? Explain.

_____
_____
_____
_____
_____
_____
_____
_____
_____
_____
_____
_____
_____
_____
_____
_____

Care for Yourself

"It's not selfish to love yourself, take care of yourself, and to make your happiness a priority. It is Necessary."
-Mandy Hale

Getting to Know Yourself | 46

1. What are your favorite self-care activities?

_____
_____
_____
_____
_____
_____
_____
_____
_____
_____
_____
_____
_____
_____
_____

2. Fill in the blank - "I feel most energized when I _____." Explain.

_____
_____
_____
_____
_____
_____
_____
_____
_____
_____
_____
_____
_____
_____
_____
_____
_____
_____

3. Do you put your well-being first or do you put others first?

_____
_____
_____
_____
_____
_____
_____
_____
_____
_____
_____
_____
_____
_____
_____

4. Are you in control of what goes on in your life? Think spiritually and earthly. Explain.

_____
_____
_____
_____
_____
_____
_____
_____
_____
_____
_____
_____
_____
_____
_____
_____

5. To what degree have you controlled the course of your life?

_____
_____
_____
_____
_____
_____
_____
_____
_____
_____
_____
_____
_____
_____
_____
_____
_____
_____

6. Are you allowing matters beyond your control to stress you? Explain.

_____
_____
_____
_____
_____
_____
_____
_____
_____
_____
_____
_____
_____
_____
_____
_____

7. Are you the person you want to be? Explain why or why not.

_____
_____
_____
_____
_____
_____
_____
_____
_____
_____
_____
_____
_____
_____
_____

8. What is worse to you, failing or never trying? Why?

_____
_____
_____
_____
_____
_____
_____
_____
_____
_____
_____
_____
_____
_____
_____

9. What are your five-year goals?

1. _____
_____
_____

2. _____
_____
_____

3. _____
_____
_____

4. _____
_____
_____

5. _____
_____
_____

10. Do you have goal deadlines? Are they realistic? Motivating? Why or why not?

_____
_____
_____
_____
_____
_____
_____
_____
_____
_____
_____
_____
_____
_____
_____
_____
_____

Love Yourself

"How you love yourself is how you teach others to love you."
-Rupi Kaur

1. What do you love about life? Why?

_____
_____
_____
_____
_____
_____
_____
_____
_____
_____
_____
_____
_____
_____
_____

2. If you could talk to your younger self, what would you say?

_____
_____
_____
_____
_____
_____
_____
_____
_____
_____
_____
_____
_____
_____
_____
_____

3. Would you break the law to save a loved one? Explain.

_____
_____
_____
_____
_____
_____
_____
_____
_____
_____
_____
_____
_____
_____
_____
_____
_____

4. What three words or phrases would you like to live by? Why?

1. _____

_____

_____

_____

_____

2. _____

_____

_____

_____

_____

3. _____

_____

_____

_____

_____

5. What couldn't you imagine your life without? Why?

_____
_____
_____
_____
_____
_____
_____
_____
_____
_____
_____
_____
_____
_____
_____
_____

6. What have you given up on that mattered to you? Why?

_____
_____
_____
_____
_____
_____
_____
_____
_____
_____
_____
_____
_____
_____
_____
_____
_____

7. Do you care how others perceive you? Why or why not?

_____
_____
_____
_____
_____
_____
_____
_____
_____
_____
_____
_____
_____
_____
_____
_____
_____
_____

8. Who do you think you are as a person? How would you like to be perceived?

_____
_____
_____
_____
_____
_____
_____
_____
_____
_____
_____
_____
_____
_____

Do You Know You? | 67

Thank you for your continued support and prayers. Look out for the next two volumes of my self-healing workbook. In this book, these questions are for you to get to know who you truly are. Many of us believe that we know ourselves when we do not. Take the time to answer these questions truthfully. Each volume becomes more intrusive, with more in-depth questions. Volume 2 you will dig deeper and will have you thinking more. Volume 3 you will reveal yourself to yourself. You will learn more and more about yourself within both of these coming volumes.

  Buckle your seat belts and get ready for this ride of healing. I am so excited for you to see what I have in store.

  Follow me on Instagram: @jazz.withabuncha.sass (Jazmine Stevenson)
  Add me on Facebook: Jazmine Stevenson
  Send me an email: jazmine.stevenson94@gmail.com
  Subscribe to my YouTube channel: RealTalkWithNonii

Please continue to spread the word, for you too can help Impact the World.

#IWILLIMPACTTHEWORLD

About the Author

Born in Brooklyn and raised in New Jersey, Jazmine Stevenson was always a vibrant little girl who loves her family and tight circle of friends. Her outgoing personality and ease in connecting with others made her a natural fit to help the elderly population and those who may have special needs. To this day, she has a unique passion for dance and making people feel great with her stupendous hugs that are unlike anyone else's.

Despite facing obstacles casting uncertainty on her collegiate prospects, through long sleepless nights and tears, Jazmine graduated from Ramapo College in 2017 with a B.A. in Social Science with a concentration in community mental health and a minor in substance abuse. In October 2021, she became certified as a lifestyle life coach. Jazmine has taken the trials she faced on the road to success and transformed them into a business brand. She plans to use her talents in order to conduct outreach and effect real change in her community, one person at a time.

www.ingramcontent.com/pod-product-compliance
Lightning Source LLC
Chambersburg PA
CBHW081755100526
44592CB00015B/2446